What Our Readers Have Said...

"The Pinpoint Training Series delivers information that could be used in a lot different areas."

•

"Applicable and valid. The information is good."

•

"I like this because I can take them with me to read at a convenient time. I feel the little time I have to spend in the office is best use on activities that directly relate to revenue opportunities. I like the short amount of time it takes to keep up with these."

•

"I like the fact that the format allows the books to be reviewed as time permits. All work has been conducted on personal, evening/weekend time."

•

"My thought is that the real value of these books comes into effect when doing the action plans."

•

"The challenge when I think a specific topic does not apply is to find a way to make it apply."

•

"Short and sweet. These books are easy to comprehend."

•

"These books are very easy to read and clearly outlined."

•

"I have enjoyed reading these books. They are relevant to today's work environment and the ongoing change in the way we manage our workforce."

•

"I believe the contents of the Pinpoint series are excellent. It causes one to reflect on the daily dynamics in working with oneself as well as with management and peers."

•

"Most of the information in these would help an open-minded management person, or an inexperienced management person."

•

"These books will pay for the time that I am investing. There are numerous good ideas that will streamline what I do and how I do it."

•

"All and all I think the Pinpoint series is a good program. I know other people I would love to have something like this. I think a lot of the suggestions are very useful, and can be applicable to everyday situations. If nothing else it's a good reference guide to fall back upon if a situation arises in the future."

•

"These books reinforce many concepts that I have learned through seminars, schooling and other programs. For myself, it serves as a constant learning tool that keeps me on top of the issues that many of us encounter every day."

•

"All in all, I think you have good training books. It helps everyone to review these materials, it serves as a good reminder to us on how to conduct ourselves."

•

"The information is valuable in these books."

•

Overcoming Management Challenges

Pinpoint Sales Management Skill Development Training Series

TIMOTHY F. BEDNARZ

MAJORIUM
BUSINESS PRESS

Pinpoint Sales Management Skill Development Training Series
"Overcoming Management Challenges"
Timothy F. Bednarz

Graphic design: Monika Pawlak

Majorium Business Press
2025 Main Street
Stevens Point, WI 54481
715.342.1018 • 800.654.4935

ISBN 978-1-62101-054-8

Printed in the United States of America

Introduction

The Pinpoint Sales Management Skill Development Training Series is designed for targeted training and education regarding increased improvement in a specific skill or competency.

Each book within this series is designed to be easy to use, understand and apply to your job. It can be used as a basis for training individuals, as a discussion guide or as a personal training tool.

Each chapter within this book discusses a specific concept. When you have completed all eight chapters you should have a 360° perspective of the topic.

Additionally, each chapter is divided into specific sections:

- The first section provides you with an overview of the topic
- The Implications section discusses why the concept is important, and why it is important to learn and apply.
- The Strategies, Tips & Techniques to Apply section teaches how to use and apply the particular concept to your work.
- The Points to Ponder section gives you something to think about or to be discussed with a group setting. These are questions not meant to be immediately answered, but to be pondered over time.
- The Training Activity section provides you with the tools to transfer what you have learned to your job. It is designed to help create an action plan to effectively apply the concept.

Each of the topics in this series is time-tested and proven in the marketplace. They have been used by thousands of employees as training tools. Many of the users have commented that what made these books valuable, was the ability to refer to them when a problem surfaced. They indicated that they remembered reading about the exact problem. They referred back to these books and found an appropriate solution.

You will find them equally valuable as a resource in your professional development library.

Table of Contents

LEARNING OBJECTIVES:

- Critical factors facing today's sales manager.
- To effectively deal with common management traps and pitfalls.
- To apply the best practices in sales management.
- To increase overall effectiveness and productivity.

1

Challenges Facing the Sales Manager

The speed and impact of the recent recessionary cycle has affected businesses in many sectors. The lingering effects have changed the complexion of the business community and will continue to do so into the future.

The way companies operate has changed, which presents sales managers with specific near-term challenges.

IMPLICATIONS — WHAT THIS MEANS TO YOU

The length and breadth of the last boom business cycle has produced a generation of sales managers who have never operated in a recessionary cycle. The suddenness of the recession took many by surprise who were thus unprepared to deal with the ramifications of the slowdown. This presents a major challenge to virtually every sales manager. The remnants of the recession—along with the events of September 11, 2001—have shocked many companies out of the free-wheeling spending habits that exemplified the 1990s. Times have changed and sales managers are presented with a distinct set of challenges that must be faced.

STRATEGIES, TIPS & TECHNIQUES TO APPLY

Sibson and Company, a major human resources consulting firm, surveyed managers and asked them to rank eight challenges that they face in improving overall performance. Several concerns are outlined below:

Reinforcing Support Systems

Improving the systems that support their salespeople is the top challenge for sales managers. Rapid deployment and flow of information to facilitate decision making, as well as the training of their people, are key support areas impacting the overall performance of the individual salesperson. Performance enhancement, especially as budgets continue to tighten, increases the salesperson's ability to ratchet up his or her individual capabilities and professional abilities in order to meet increased challenges of current market conditions.

Realigning Internal Processes

Sales managers are faced with the challenges of realigning the processes within their organization to address the changes in buying criteria and processes. Buyers are more sophisticated, and the buying process has appreciably lengthened over the past several years. Additionally, the impact of the past recessionary cycle has changed not only the way many companies buy, but also promises to make changes in how they view purchasing in the future.

Strengthening Salespeople's Understanding of Customer Profit Economics

While customer knowledge has always been one of the pillars of success, sales managers are faced with the challenge of educating their sales teams about their customer's profit economics and how their specific products or services not only fit into that equation, but also how they impact overall profitability.

The sobering effects of the past recessionary cycle have shaken many companies out of boom-time buying patterns. Companies are now looking closely at the cost of a purchase and its impact on their investment. Products and services that are not delivering an adequate ROI are being closely scrutinized and in many cases eliminated in favor of better-performing products or services.

Reconstructing and Realigning Reward Programs

Specific salesperson behaviors are significantly impacted by how those behaviors are financially rewarded. As companies move toward strategies that enhance customer retention and the development of partnering relationships with their customers, compensation plans must be revised to align salespeople behaviors with these desired outcomes.

Sales managers are challenged to develop compensation plans that reward the desired behaviors while meeting the overall goals of the company.

Flattening Decision Making

Sales managers are challenged to move the daily decisions they typically make directly to their frontline people. Salespeople are thus given the latitude to make quick and timely decisions "on the fly" that can positively impact the speed and quality of results. This process frees the sales manager to spend more time on strategic and productive tasks that impact the overall performance of their department or unit.

Strengthening Salespeople's Understanding of Their Companies' Profit Economics

Before decision making can be effectively flattened, salespeople must be educated to understand and apply specific knowledge of their company's own profit economics. Without a complete understanding of the profit margins and cost of delivering a product or service, salespeople are unable to make critical decisions.

Additionally, the application of this knowledge can be directly linked to the compensation plan. An element to be considered is the level of profitability and return on investment a salesperson can provide from the work he or she is doing. Rewards and bonuses can be directly linked to increased profit levels of future work.

POINTS TO PONDER – SOMETHING TO THINK ABOUT

1. What challenges have you unexpectedly faced in the past 18-24 months?
2. What challenges do you anticipate this upcoming year?

TRAINING ACTIVITY – APPLICATION & ACTION PLAN

Under each of the items listed below identify the specific challenges that face your organization and how you might overcome each one.

- Reinforcing Salesperson Support Systems
- Realigning Internal Processes
- Strengthening Salespeople' Understanding of Customer Profit Economics
- Reconstructing and Realigning Reward Programs
- Flattening Decision Making
- Strengthening Salespeople' Understanding of Their Companies' Profit Economics

2

Critical Factors in Sales Management

Sales managers must confront and overcome many barriers and challenges. There are a number of interconnected factors that both impact outcomes and present a new set of challenges. The goal is to understand these connections and realize how one solution relates to another.

IMPLICATIONS — WHAT THIS MEANS TO YOU

Sales managers are facing an increasingly uphill battle as they encounter more challenges and pressures than in the past. The complex mix of economic conditions and volatility that all businesses have had to contend with during recent years has only complicated the situation.

It is important for sales managers to understand the changing business climate because these challenges can be daunting, if not overwhelming. Sales managers must take a systematic approach by breaking each challenge into manageable sections and then digesting them in small chunks. Otherwise it is too easy for them to become consumed with problem solving, which detracts from their primary responsibility of moving their unit/department forward and meeting the goals of the company.

STRATEGIES, TIPS & TECHNIQUES TO APPLY

Sales managers are unquestionably facing a more difficult time than ever before. During the 90s the business cycle was in an upturn and company growth was relatively easy to achieve. The sudden downturn took many by surprise and has resulted in dramatic shifts in the way business is conducted. This difference not only complicates the sales manager's life, but also increases the challenges they must overcome in the following areas:

Economy

The softness and volatility of the economy presents a real challenge to many sales managers, especially those in lagging industries such as paper and advertising.

Some salespeople are learning to adapt to changes in operating conditions, but many are still lagging in performance while blaming economic conditions. Sales managers are called upon to motivate their salespeople to readily adapt and generate the desired outcomes that meet both their unit's and company's goals and objectives.

Change

Change was a factor even before the recent economic downturn and will continue to be an issue for sales managers. In addition to problems that technological advancement brings to a business and industry, the recent recession has changed the way many companies now operate in relation to their vendors and suppliers. People are taking a much closer look at the ROI that a specific product or service brings to their business. Many frivolous and luxurious purchases are being eliminated or replaced with more frugal items.

Customer Retention

Securing the business base has taken on increased importance to companies in lagging economic conditions. Sales managers are realizing that the best source of new business lies in the opportunities that existing customers provide for expanding product use and new product applications. A study by Harvard

Business School reported that a 2% retention rate of existing customers is equal to a 10% reduction in operating expenses.

Cultivation of Ideas

As important as customer retention is to the salespeople, sales managers are equally challenged to motivate their people to generate new ideas for cutting costs and building profitability. As business conditions continue to lag, many salespeople are experiencing frustrations with new projects and purchases that are placed on indefinite hold until business conditions firm up. However, sales managers must keep their sales teams focused, and direct their efforts toward alternative ideas and projects.

Motivation

Motivating the individual salesperson is an ongoing issue for sales managers even in the best of times, but is an increased challenge during economic downturns. Many individuals have never experienced operating during a time of recession, and this requires a different skill set than selling in robust times.

Sales managers are challenged to maintain motivation, which can be accomplished by additional training and coaching to help salespeople work more effectively and efficiently under more difficult economic conditions.

Service

The existing trend to provide heightened levels of service continues to grow as customers are becoming more demanding and extremely cost conscious. As people are seeking more effective and customized solutions to resolve specific problems, they increasingly form economic partnerships to share the risks. Sales managers are pushed to grow more flexible in meeting customer demands.

Resource Utilization

Sales managers will need to take a closer look at the resources available to them. This might mean a realignment of internal processes and procedures to best serve changing customer needs.

Results

Sales managers must continue to produce the results required of them by senior management. Sales managers are often placed in a difficult position of meeting greater goals and objectives while dealing with declining performance and motivation brought on by lagging economic conditions. It is a precarious position for any sales manager to be placed in. They must balance the demands of the company with the needs of their salespeople and customers.

POINTS TO PONDER – SOMETHING TO THINK ABOUT

1. What additional factors increase your challenges as a sales manager?
2. What factors do you see as your highest priority?

TRAINING ACTIVITY – APPLICATION & ACTION PLAN

1. List the following factors on a sheet of paper and include under each the specific challenges that you must meet.
2. Identify possible solutions next to each challenge and the best course of action to follow to meet and overcome it.
    - Economy
    - Change
    - Customer Retention
    - Cultivation of Ideas
    - Motivation
    - Service
    - Resource Utilization
    - Results

3

How's Today's Challenges Impact Management

The impact of today's challenges on sales managers is enormous and unprecedented in recent memory, as people adapt to economic volatility and related changes in business conditions. Most sales managers are faced with unforeseen challenges and are baffled regarding how to handle them.

IMPLICATIONS – WHAT THIS MEANS TO YOU

The challenges facing sales managers are directly related to the changing economic conditions and the need for most organizations to reinvent themselves in the face of dramatic change.

Sales managers need to be aware of the situation because market conditions will not return to the "Clinton economic bubble" of the 90s. The economic paradigm has changed and sales managers must affect a pivotal shift in their own thinking if they wish to adapt their organizations to these changes. Without a shift in focus they will experience increased ineffectiveness, as well as a loss of salesperson productivity and overall profitability.

STRATEGIES, TIPS & TECHNIQUES TO APPLY

A critical review and analysis of the specific challenges facing the sales manager today pinpoints two major areas and their ramifications for an organization. The areas to be focused on include the economy and change. Both of these factors are closely interlinked because the dramatic changes concurrent with the economic volatility of the early 2000s have completely changed the complexion of selling.

Upon examination of the specific challenges facing sales managers, the following list of goals was defined:

- Reinforcing Salesperson Support Systems
- Realigning Internal Processes
- Strengthening Salespeople's Understanding of Customer Profit Economics
- Reconstructing and Realigning Reward Programs
- Flattening Decision Making
- Strengthening Salespeople's Understanding of Their Companies' Profit Economics

Sales managers responding to the changes that the volatile economy has produced singled out the above issues as being most critical. More importantly, identification of these challenges displays a conscious effort on the part of sales managers to adapt and modify methods and procedures to match the shifts experienced in the marketplace.

The methods employed during the Clinton years are nearly obsolete today. For sales managers, the implications of this change are enormous. When examining the critical factors in management, virtually every area is affected by these recent economic changes. These factors are:

- Economy
- Change
- Customer Retention
- Cultivation of Ideas

- Motivation
- Service
- Resource Utilization
- Results

A profound shift in the manner in which products and services are sold has taken place, which is further complicated by the fact that many current salespeople gained their experience during the 90s. Most of the seasoned salespeople who worked through the "misery index" of the Carter years are no longer in the profession to share their expertise. Consequently, as economic history repeats itself, most sales managers and salespeople have to learn valuable lessons all over again. The problem facing most sales managers lies in the fact that these are costly lessons to learn.

This process is further complicated by the fact that the continued volatility of the marketplace does not provide a clear focus of direction for organizations. Continued volatility means that customer behavior will fluctuate until economic conditions finally begin to stabilize. As a result, changes implemented today may be obsolete in several months.

Sales managers are making more decisions under uncertainty, meaning that the risks associated with every decision must be carefully considered and evaluated. This also has implications for how customers conduct their business. Since they are also making decisions under uncertainty, the customer is exposed to risk and is thus more cautious, which can impact what they purchase. This uncertainty lengthens the sales cycle and influences future purchasing levels.

The bottom line is that the challenges facing sales managers are forcing them to reevaluate their business-as-usual approach that may no longer be working in the marketplace. Whether or not sales managers want to, they must change. A major consequence of the existing challenges is that sales managers must reinvent how to produce, market and sell their products or services. The primary concern that they must address is how they can help the company compete effectively during times of uncertainty. As customers strive to reduce risks to their business, they become more focused on the ROI of each investment they make. An organization must demonstrate the economic benefits that they can deliver.

POINTS TO PONDER – SOMETHING TO THINK ABOUT

1. What changes have you experienced that are challenging your organization?
2. What is the biggest challenge you are facing?

TRAINING ACTIVITY – APPLICATION & ACTION PLAN

Get "out of the box" and begin to view your product or service from the customer's perspective.

1. Identify the economic benefits that your product or service can offer.
2. Determine whether your product or service is critical to the customer's success or is more of a luxury.
3. Identify ways to clearly and concisely communicate the economic benefit of your product, especially in volatile economic times.

4

Avoiding Management Traps and Pitfalls

Surmounting barriers and overcoming the daunting challenges facing sales managers in a volatile marketplace can be a real problem. These stumbling blocks can easily lead sales managers into unexpected traps and pitfalls. Due to the nature of complex challenges, sales managers must take particular care to avoid their negative ramifications.

IMPLICATIONS — WHAT THIS MEANS TO YOU

Coping with the complexity of challenges facing today's sales manager can be a major job unto itself. Squeezing valuable time from an already hectic schedule to address problems associated with challenges can easily lead many sales managers into pitfalls that can have far-reaching consequences.

When dealing with daily occurrences and problems, most sales managers are forced into a tactical thinking mode: certain circumstances demand their immediate attention, and they have little time other than to quickly react and solve the problem as smoothly and efficiently as possible. Consequently, many sales managers fail to exercise strategic, systematic thinking to deal with and overcome sudden challenges.

Strategic thinking should be prioritized and include complex, cause-and-effect reasoning. Without thinking strategically, additional problems and issues will begin to surface that only complicate the challenges to be surmounted.

STRATEGIES, TIPS & TECHNIQUES TO APPLY

The ramifications confronting the current set of challenges can be perilous and must be carefully analyzed. Due to the volatility and fluctuation of the marketplace, sales managers can find themselves stumbling into the following pitfalls:

A Business-as-Usual Mindset

One of the most dangerous traps for a sales manager is to only draw insight from and rely on their usual thinking patterns and habits. Those people who have been seasoned during more robust economic times generally have a tendency to believe that conditions will gradually improve and that past conditions will be restored; however, indications are that such thinking is invalid.

The speed of the economic downturn, exacerbated by the terrorist attacks of September 11, 2001, suggest that most businesses will not return to the market conditions prior to the burst of the "Clinton economic bubble." The above factors have caused many customers to rethink their business methods, decision paths and purchasing habits. All indicators point to a paradigm shift in the way business will be conducted in the future. Sales managers who think otherwise are being shortsighted, and are unprepared to develop proactive and offensive strategies that take advantage of emerging opportunities or overcome slumps and dips in current business accounts.

Failure to Closely Monitor Market Conditions and Trends

The pace of change and the continuous volatility of the marketplace indicate that many companies are struggling to adapt to changing market conditions. Further, there are indications that the pace and complexity of change will continue for some time to come.

A pitfall for sales managers is to assume that the existing changes in economic conditions will continue, when in fact no one really knows if the market will grow or decline. Rather than make assumptions about the future, sales managers must closely monitor current market conditions and trends until the economy stabilizes; this is the only way for sales managers to capitalize on opportunities and avert potential problems.

A failure to adequately monitor the situation can result in an organization being blindsided by future market conditions, events and circumstances. Obviously, no one can predict terrorist attacks of the magnitude of those on September 11, 2001, but conditions indicate there will be continued attacks. Sales managers are best prepared by asking themselves a series of "what-if" questions to anticipate the future consequences of unforeseen and uncontrollable events on their business.

Failure to Adapt

The specific actions listed below are examples of how sales managers can adapt their organizations to the changes they are facing in the marketplace:

- Reinforce Sales Support Systems
- Realign Internal Processes
- Strengthen Salespeople's Understanding of Customer Profit Economics
- Reconstruct and Realign Reward Programs
- Flatten Decision Making
- Strengthen Salespeople's Understanding of Their Companies' Profit Economics

Each one of the above challenges identified by sales managers has a direct impact on the way each sales manager must lead his or her team. Effective sales managers must recognize the need for change or they will face the consequences of not meeting and addressing the developing needs of their salespeople and organization.

Failure to Commit to Continuous Improvement and Change

Change is dynamic and continuous. A typical pitfall for many sales managers is to make static changes and then ignore the subsequent impact on their organization. Often accompanying this misstep is a sales manager's failure to recognize that change is perpetual, and that any adaptations they make must be both dynamic and flexible to meet the changing market conditions their salespeople will encounter. Sales managers must develop a program that monitors the impact of change, and they must continually apply this system to make any necessary modifications warranted by market conditions. During more stagnant conditions, these changes may be frequent; as conditions stabilize, fluctuations might occur less often.

POINTS TO PONDER — SOMETHING TO THINK ABOUT

1. What additional pitfalls or traps do you feel you need to avoid?
2. How do you balance tactical thinking with strategic thinking?

TRAINING ACTIVITY — APPLICATION & ACTION PLAN

Create a program or system for yourself that allows you to:

1. Identify the specific challenges facing your unit/department.
2. Identify future opportunities and ways to avoid potential problems.
3. Commit to a program of continuous improvement and change.

5

Best Practices in Sales Management

It is not only important for sales managers to recognize the challenges that they will face, but also to understand how to meet and overcome such trials. Preparation provides them with a starting point and the impetus to change.

IMPLICATIONS – WHAT THIS MEANS TO YOU

As the complexity and depth of challenges increase, sales managers cannot afford to ignore the issues that currently confront them. Doing so will create a domino effect of problems that will continue to plague them until dealt with. More importantly, sales managers will learn that the obstacles, barriers and challenges to their business will continue at an alarming rate, fueled by technological advancements and changes in the global economy.

Cognizant of the above circumstances, sales managers can devote more time to meeting the strategic challenges that continue to confront their business. At the same time, more of the tactical issues must be pushed to the frontline salesperson. The strategic nature of many challenges precludes most sales managers from micromanaging the activities of their people and forces them to deal with the macro-issues of management.

STRATEGIES, TIPS & TECHNIQUES TO APPLY

Under each of the items listed below, there are specific strategies sales managers can employ to meet challenges.

Reinforcing Salesperson Support Systems

The rapid flow of information between sales managers and their salespeople is the biggest challenge to be faced. It is recommended that sales managers conduct a complete reassessment of their salesperson support system. The best approach is to flowchart the entire system so as to completely understand its methodology and complexity. Over time, support systems tend to become increasingly complex and redundant as new elements are put into place, which overburdens the process.

Sales managers should consider a complete redesign of their support systems; this can start with a fresh set of goals and objectives to use as a foundation. With these goals and objectives in mind, sales managers should analyze the type and form of information that both they and their salespeople require, and the best means of obtaining and delivering that information. The key is to remember that most sales managers and salespeople are awash in information, but starving for knowledge. Sales managers should look for the best methods possible to deliver knowledge over information, providing support data and information if it needs to be referenced. Some vital areas to examine are:

- The effective use of performance metrics to evaluate work.
- The conversion of reports into action plans.
- The minimization of data flow to eliminate information overload.

Realigning Internal Processes

Sales managers must conduct a comprehensive analysis of the buying habits and patterns of their customer base. As buyers become more sophisticated and are forced to face the realities of increased global competition and a depressed economy, their behaviors change. Sales managers must examine and monitor these changes, and analyze future trends: when compared to their existing processes, most will find profound shifts. The impact of the Internet on information gathering must be addressed along with the overall increase in risk factors that change the way companies handle their purchasing. The key is to realign the internal processes using all of the available tools and technologies to closely match customers' buying behavior and to maximize the use of their people's time and resources.

The business landscape is evolving and changing. It is important to monitor these changes and continually adapt and modify the operating processes accordingly.

Strengthening Salespeople's Understanding of Customer Profit Economics

There is no doubt that the many changes of the early 2000s have precipitated a shift in customer economics. If anything, the recent impact of the recession combined with the global terrorist risks have induced many companies to re-evaluate the manner in which they conduct business. Companies are purchasing more carefully and examining the return on investment a specific product or service delivers to them. Consequently, unless salespeople understand the economics of their business and how their product or service fits into that picture, they will be quickly discounted.

Sales managers should require their people to conduct a review of their companies' major accounts in order to understand the specific application of their product or service, recognize the importance of that product or service to the customer, and glean how the product directly contributes to the customer's profitability. Only when salespeople know how their product contributes to customer success can they successfully position themselves to contribute to the bottom line.

Reconstructing and Realigning Reward Programs

As companies realign their internal processes and require more servicing of accounts, sales managers must adjust their compensation plans to reflect these changes. Compensation plans should be designed so that salespeople perform desired activities and functions, which can include business development and service. Research shows that salespeople will gravitate to where they are making the most money. If they are paid on commission it is unlikely service will be important to them.

Sales managers should identify and prioritize desired behaviors. Based upon what they come up with they will have a platform for creating a compensation program that meets their goals.

Flattening Decision Making

Sales managers are challenged to move the decisions typically made by sales managers directly to their frontline people. Salespeople are thus given the latitude to make quick and timely operational decisions that can positively impact the speed and quality of results.

Strengthening Salespeople's Understanding of Their Companies' Profit Economics

Salespeople should be educated in the profit margins of the products/services their company sells. They need to understand the impact an order has on their business as well as the financial ramifications of customer concessions. Once furnished with this information, their performance should be evaluated not only on their specific work-related activities, but also on the profitability of the portion of business for which they are responsible.

POINTS TO PONDER — SOMETHING TO THINK ABOUT

1. What additional strategies can be utilized by your organization to meet existing challenges?
2. Which strategies offered above do you feel might not be workable?

TRAINING ACTIVITY – APPLICATION & ACTION PLAN

Develop a flow chart of your existing salesperson support system. Then, chart a system that you feel best meets the needs of your people. Compare and contrast the two.

1. Determine what is working the best and develop a plan to build on this level of performance.
2. Determine what is ineffective and eliminate it.
3. Fine-tune your flow chart into a workable salesperson support plan.

6

When Challenges are Left Unmet

Sales managers are overwhelmed and burdened with many tasks and responsibilities in a constant quest to improve results. It is easy for sales managers to ignore the many challenges that confront them while hoping that issues will resolve themselves. However, rather than disappear, unmet challenges create a new set of problems that can represent a deepening morass from which sales managers must extricate themselves.

IMPLICATIONS — WHAT THIS MEANS TO YOU

Problems and challenges are a regular and ongoing occurrence: some surface as daily tactical problems and issues, while others are more complex, time-consuming and strategic in nature. In all forms, problems can overwhelm the sales manager and sap their productivity.

Sales managers must create a systematic approach to problem solving to allow time for their regular duties and responsibilities. Without a detailed, time-focused approach that allows sales managers to break challenges down into more manageable components, they will quickly feel overwhelmed by the enormousness of the demands facing them.

STRATEGIES, TIPS & TECHNIQUES TO APPLY

The sales manager who hopes that problems will go away on their own will be faced with the following consequences:

Closely Controlled Information

The flow and control of critical information is a management issue. Many sales managers base their personal power on how they manage and control information made available to their salespeople. Yet the free-flow of information to frontline salespeople is essential for success. Sales managers who attempt to micromanage their salespeople and limit the information fed to them, contribute to undermining the efficiency of the sales team.

Salespeople are hindered when they are not given the information they need to be competitive. Without the information and authority to make decisions on the spot, their efforts can be negatively impacted by delays. When decisions are pushed up the line for sales managers to make, bottlenecks are often created and critical decisions are not made in a timely manner; potential results include lost productivity or poor customer service. At a time when customers are increasingly demanding, this can be extremely problematic. Rather than make salespeople more effective by streamlining the process, sales managers often erect additional barriers that hinder performance.

Loss of Critical Skills

In response to slow economic conditions, many companies cut their discretionary spending and slash training budgets. Rather than focus on the development of skills that can have a direct bearing on the success of a company, many allow skills to become outmoded and ineffective during slow periods. Consequently, companies experience an additional decline in performance, which then necessitate further cuts.

Rather than focus on reducing training budgets, sales managers should seek to sharpen salesperson skills to achieve the same objectives. Studies have shown that a 2% increase in customer retention over the previous year's performance levels will result in a 10% reduction in operating expenses. This is due to the additional retained business impacts of economies of scale.

Disconnection Between Company and Customer Base

With the changes in purchasing habits of customers and a closer examination of the roles and returns that specific products or services offer sales managers, those who fail to meet critical challenges can find themselves increasingly disconnected from their customer base.

Salespeople who fail to understand their clients' profit economies and who are not attuned to the rapidly shifting complexion of business will find it increasingly difficult to meet their customers' needs. As companies neglect training, they rob their people of critical skills at the apex of change.

Inefficient Use of Resources

Not only are companies more demanding, but the use of various new methods and technologies have made for more diverse methods of collecting and disseminating information. The use of face-to-face meetings is in many circumstances no longer the most efficient use of resources. The use of the phone and web conferencing can supplement traditional meetings and free sales managers to pursue more essential activities.

Additionally, if sales managers fail to focus on the desired outcomes of their business processes and the behaviors required to achieve those goals, they are, once again, inefficiently using their resources. Failure to align desired behaviors and goals with compensation plans will result in a failure to meet objectives and negatively impact the organization.

Minimizing Profit Potential

The failure to meet new and ongoing challenges through heightened training can result in the minimization of profit potential. Salespeople who do not understand the profit economics of their products/services cannot comprehend how they might impact and improve the profitability of their own efforts.

Deterioration of Growth

Sales managers who neglect to deal with a new problem are either in denial of the situation or hope it will resolve itself. However, a failure to meet challenges will create a domino effect across the entire organization. All challenges are interconnected: each impacts the other. If solutions are not addressed in tandem, they risk failing. Consequently, when sales managers fail to meet the issues facing them head on, they can easily undermine their unit and organization's growth. The hazard is always present, but the consequences manifest themselves in increments, and the impact is only truly felt over time.

POINTS TO PONDER — SOMETHING TO THINK ABOUT

1. What are your personal feelings toward meeting challenges?
2. Do you ignore changes and hope they will disappear on their own?

TRAINING ACTIVITY — APPLICATION & ACTION PLAN

Identify the challenges you face that you are most reluctant to tackle.

1. Pinpoint the reasons behind your reluctance.
2. Determine the validity of your reasoning.
3. Explore strategies to overcome your reluctance.
4. Break the challenge into manageable pieces.
5. Work on one piece of the issue at a time until the entire challenge is overcome.

7

How Management Challenges Impacts Decision Making

Sales managers facing today's challenges specifically identify a number of critical factors to be vigilant for when it comes to business operation. Sales managers must become familiar with and use these factors in their decision making process. A failure to adjust will result in shallow and faulty decisions and often cause salespeople to be blindsided by uncontrollable events and circumstances.

IMPLICATIONS – WHAT THIS MEANS TO YOU

Undoubtedly, the roles and responsibilities of the sales manager have evolved in the face of increased global competition and the multitude of changes experienced by companies over the past 10-15 years. Since sales managers have the primary responsibility of increasing the overall results of their unit, it is easy for many to be myopic—rather than global and strategic—in their outlook.

Sales managers must understand that as the complexity of business has changed, so has the face of selling. Yet many have failed to keep pace with these fluctuations. This failure can be seen in the use of outmoded managing techniques that are still utilized by more than two-thirds of companies. While the face of business has changed, many companies and their people are still using manipulative management methods popular more than 30 years ago. As an indicator of adaptation to change, if companies have failed to modify their management methodology, what other elements have they also failed to adjust? Rather than be reactive, sales managers must be proactive by coming up with unique ways to better accomplish their goals and objectives.

STRATEGIES, TIPS & TECHNIQUES TO APPLY

Sales managers must develop a mindset that is more strategic and global, as well as tactical, in nature. Events and circumstances once evaluated only by senior management are increasingly being dealt with at lower levels in organizations. As companies flatten decision making and push decisions to their people "in the trenches," the breadth and scope of information required by sales managers and salespeople increases. Sales managers must now consider the following factors and include them in their decisions:

Global Changes

Global changes that were once considered to be of strategic importance to senior management are now impacting companies and individuals in the most rural communities heretofore isolated from the rest of the world. The ramifications of this shift are enormous and must be considered as part of every sales manager's decision making process. Obviously, these global changes affect companies and regions differently, but there is no doubt that all sales managers must be aware of them. They must realize how their company's customers are impacted, and should be prepared to adapt their salespeople accordingly in order to meet these realities.

Impact of Technology

A consequence of globalization is an increase in the use and application of technology in every facet of business. Companies are continually striving to do things faster, better and cheaper. These changes impact all businesses throughout the world and must be seriously considered by every sales manager. New and more efficient technologies can quickly devastate any marketplace, regardless of how secure it may have seemed. The key is for sales managers to anticipate how these trends ultimately impact their salespeople as well as overall company performance.

Economy

The world is clearly shrinking, and the impact of economic conditions on business is increasingly being felt both locally and globally. The value of the dollar against foreign currencies affects prices and product availability. Sales managers must appreciate and factor these realities into their decision making process. Nothing exists in a void: all companies are impacted by world events and economic conditions either directly or indirectly via prospects and customers. Without an understanding of how world economic events and conditions affect his or her company and its customers, the sales manager lacks sufficient knowledge to make informed decisions.

Competition

Every company and individual sales manager reacts to the same set of facts in a different way. Sales managers must understand their competition's position and decisions in order to anticipate how they should respond to specific challenges. Some may have the strength to weather an economic storm, while others will react wildly and erratically in an attempt to survive. Sales managers who employ critical thinking skills that anticipate competitive moves and strategies can shield their own portion of the business from taking a hit.

Customer Dynamics

Salespeople will also react in different manners to the same set of circumstances and events. Both sales managers and their people must have specific insight into their customers' businesses and thinking, without which they will not be in the proper position to capitalize on opportunities.

Company Dynamics

In like regard, sales managers must have full insight into the dynamics of their own company in its response to challenges. Without this knowledge sales managers cannot align their own goals and objectives with the company's, and they run the risk of undermining and even negating corporate initiatives.

Individual Salesperson Behaviors

The final factor a sales manager must take into account is how the preceding elements impact individual salesperson behavior. In doing this, sales managers must take their macro-thinking and apply it on a micro-level where it impacts the salesperson. There must be transference of knowledge so that salespeople can understand how these strategic and global elements ultimately impact them individually.

POINTS TO PONDER — SOMETHING TO THINK ABOUT

1. To what degree have you been strategic and global in making decisions?
2. Do you fully understand the impact and ramification of these factors on your individual business?

TRAINING ACTIVITY — APPLICATION & ACTION PLAN

1. Consider your knowledge in each of the following areas:
    - Global Changes
    - Impact of Technology
    - Economy
    - Competition
    - Customer Dynamics
    - Company Dynamics
    - Individual Salesperson Behaviors

2. Determine the areas that you are personally weak in and develop strategies to broaden your knowledge.
3. Make sure that you understand the specific impact and ramifications that each factor has upon your business and organization.
4. Communicate that information with your team on a regular basis.

8

Surmounting Challenges

As challenges are met and surmounted, sales managers will experience an evolution in both their organization and in their individual roles. However, since the solutions to specific challenges can be incremental, it is often difficult to measure overall progress by identifying specific milestones and understanding their individual significance.

IMPLICATIONS – WHAT THIS MEANS TO YOU

As sales managers confront various challenges, they will see themselves adapting as the organization adjusts to the forces of change. The sales managerial role of "control and direct" will evolve into one of "facilitator of change." Rather than micro-direct their people, sales managers will increasingly see their role on a macro-level, allowing salespeople to make more independent decisions in response to business demands and requirements.

Salespeople must understand that the challenges they overcome and surmount today will eventually be replaced by a new series of issues more complex and daunting than ever before. These changes will demand new skills, knowledge and expertise as the role of the sales manager evolves along with the company and both adapt to the changes and challenges presented. What was once considered the responsibility of the sales manager will more often be delegated to the individual salesperson. Consequently, the salesperson will not only be responsible for their own performance, but also the management of the resources assigned to him or her.

STRATEGIES, TIPS & TECHNIQUES TO APPLY

There are several specific milestones that indicate that the sales manager has made progress in meeting and surmounting the specific challenges they face. While solutions can be immediately implemented, their success may take time to measure, since progress may appear in incremental stages. This section provides sales managers with the milestones to look for.

Increase in Salesperson Effectiveness & Productivity

As market conditions change and technology impacts the organization at several levels, the best indicator of progress toward meeting goals and overcoming challenges is an increase in salesperson productivity. This increase can be the result of several key changes implemented by the sales manager, including better training, which teaches salespeople the techniques to meet the demands and needs of their jobs without utilizing outmoded manipulative methods still practiced by many companies.

Additionally, increased understanding of how to identify and meet the changing needs of their jobs enhances overall effectiveness, especially when linked with heightened levels of business knowledge. Salespeople who are more knowledgeable, who have developed specific expertise and have free access to information are also able to become more effective.

Better Utilization of Resources

Sales managers who adapt their internal processes and understand the dynamics of the business can maximize the use of their resources by tailor-making applications and aligning them with the way customers purchase goods and services. The use of intranets and call centers, along with a modification in the individual activities of salespeople can streamline the use of time and financial resources; thus, the profit potential and ROI for the unit are maximized.

More Responsive Salespeople

The flattening of decision making and the realignment of compensation and rewards will result in a unit or department that is more responsive to the organization's and customer's needs. Customer satisfaction is increased through better levels of value-added service and attention to detail, which enhances customer retention and results in a subsequent impact on the bottom line associated with higher retention rates.

Better Overall Decision Making

When decision making is flattened and driven down in the organization to the frontline salesperson, better decisions are made where they count. An increase in the level of customer responsiveness follows, which in turn yields greater overall customer satisfaction.

The whole process is enhanced by a free-flow of information to the salesperson and back to the organization. This increase in levels of valuable, first-hand information augments the quality of decisions at all levels of the organization

More Adaptive Organization

As sales managers make organizational changes to meet the challenges confronting them today, they are also putting in place systems and programs that make the organization more adaptive to future changes. Since more decision making is placed in the hands of frontline people—combined with an increased flow of information—the daily decisions that create change have a substantial impact, namely with the customer. As the needs and demands of the business evolve, the organization and the company are able to readily adapt to meet them.

Increase in Profitability

The net result of a sales manager's ability to meet the challenges facing him or her is an overall and sustainable increase in profitability. This increase is attributable to an enhancement in the individual salesperson's knowledge of the profit economics and dynamics of their company as well as the implementation of systems and programs that increase the effective utilization of resources. While the result is a consequence of the sales manager's actions, the main focus should remain on increasing the salesperson's overall productivity.

POINTS TO PONDER — SOMETHING TO THINK ABOUT

1. What prevents you from meeting and overcoming the challenges you face?
2. Are there any other indicators of progress not presented in this lesson that apply to your business?

TRAINING ACTIVITY — APPLICATION & ACTION PLAN

1. Using the following indicators, measure your organization's progress toward meeting its challenges:
    - Increase in Salesperson Effectiveness & Productivity
    - Better Utilization of Resources
    - More Responsive Salespeople
    - Better Overall Decision Making
    - More Adaptive Organization
    - Increase in Profitability
2. Identify any obstacles and barriers that appear to be blocking progress toward these goals.
3. Identify strategies to overcome and eliminate these barriers.

About the Author

Timothy F. Bednarz, Ph.D. is CEO of the American Management Development Group, Inc. For over 20 years he has researched, designed and authored hundreds of learning and development programs used by Fortune 1000 companies.

He is also the author of *Great! What Makes Leaders Great. What They Did, How They Did It and What You Can Learn from It* (2011).

Speaking Availability

Timothy F. Bednarz, Ph.D. is available for speaking engagements for your next meeting or association event. He can be contacted at 800-654-4935 or by e-mail at timothy.bednarz@majorium.com.

Bulk Sales

Bulk sales of this book or any other titles available from Majorium Business Press. Inquiries can be directed to sales@majorium.com, or by phone at 800-6654-4935.

Quick Order Form

Fax orders: 715-342-1118. Send this form.

Telephone orders: Call 800-654-4935 toll-free. Have your credit card ready.

Email orders: sales@majorium.com

Postal orders: Majorium Business Press, 2025 Main Street, Stevens Point, WI 54481, USA.

Please send the following books:

____

____

____

____

Please send more FREE information on:

❑Catalog ❑Speaking/Seminars ❑Mailing Lists ❑Consulting

Name: ____

Address: ____

City: ____________________________ State: _____ Zip: __________

Telephone: ____

Email address: ____

Sales tax: Please add 5.5% for products shipped to Wisconsin addresses.

Shipping by air:

United States: $4.00 for first book and $2.00 for each additional product.

International: $9.00 for first book; $5.00 for each additional product (estimate).

Made in United States
Cleveland, OH
05 November 2026

47664324R00030